After The Storm

Date of Publication:
September 2002

Published by:
Currock Press
3 Sandal Cliff
Sandal
Wakefield
WF2 6AU

© Copyright John Clarke

Printed by:
ProPrint
Riverside Cottage
Great North Road
Stibbington
Peterborough PE8 6LR

ISBN: 0-9543373-0-1

After The Storm

Poems By

John Clarke

Currock Press

This book is dedicated to my father
and the memory of my mother.

Thanks are extended to Michael Yates and the Black Horse
Poets (Wakefield) and also to Julie for her constant support
and encouragement.

Cover photograph © Guzelian

CONTENTS

KICKING UP

Remember when we used to stay behind
In the schoolyard for a thirty minute game?
"You, you, you and you are on ours and kicking up"
Used to be good then,
The big boys let me take the corners.
I lifted them and floated them away from the girls' toilet wall
- as real as any Wembley goal.
Darkness put an end to the second half
"See you tomorrow" fulfilled all formalities.
Running home to hide from the dark and the cold,
My breath transformed to the steam of a train
Or a kettle, or smoke from a newly lit cigarette.
By the fire in the kitchen at last
"Where have you been? And look at your shoes!"
"Sorry Mam, but we were Carlisle United."
And we won again.

BEACH FOOTBALL

I

"Play on!" is the command
 run, jump, attack, defend
So glories arise on level sand
from frantic sport played end to end
Skills performed with zeal and zest
and "bags that I be Georgie Best."

Between folded coats they make their mark
but these boys of summer will be denied
by a counter offensive after dark
and a rising swell from deep offside
Time and tide's inevitable creep
sweeps the beach while opponents sleep.

II

"Watch this, Dad!" skills displayed
polished, honed, relayed
This is where they belong
where mad dogs gad and grey waves crash
Till autumn lighting fades
on two generations at their song.

III

On Bridlington front
where it's nice to get out if you can
old men will turn on benches and say
it was different in my day
Now banner headlines shout the score
"Striker says, I'll quit"
and the Yorkshire Belle sets sail
determined in her way
then fading in the bay.

BRIGHTER THAN THE SUN

Under a blue sky children scream
on broad acres of burned grass
chasing, running, racing.
Tee-shirts show their favours
Chicago Bears and Superbowl
and protected faces are streaked with block.
"We've got to have a winner"
Aussie trainer claims
"We're skinning them alive."
Stumps pitched, field set
the boys are playing.
August the sixth, '95.

A town neglected till
Little Boy arrives
collecting souls to save more lives
one hundred and twenty thousand at a drop.
Following a flash brighter than the sun
wind burns and rain falls black
in charred remains the seeds are sown.
August the sixth, '45.

COMFORTABLE WORDS

Stones lie
neglected
in the graveyard.
Here the desperate, hopeful
messages are engraved:
Reunited and Living Redeemer.
Here, Shane or Denise
chose to spray
protestations of eternal love.

In columns of inches
page after page
of the qualities
carry the commitment
of Snuggle Buns for Cuddly
and Bear for Super Squirrel.
Till all the seas run dry.

Vomit on the carpet
caused by a cough?
At nearly four years of age
he rationalises cause and effect,
caught in the torment of expressing
the unexpressable.
His mother, aching through his illness,
embraced in incoherent,
inarticulate love.

WINTER SOLSTICE IN THE PARK

The afternoon light is on dimmer switch,
And conversation fades with dissipated breath.
Circumnavigating the reservoir
Step by step the footsteps fall.
Late leisurely walkers have taken to their hearths,
And staring geese parade
Their uniform indifference.

Step by step the footsteps fall.
Completing the final climb, the final slope,
To be blinded by a burnished gold medallion
Sinking below the horizon,
A father and son are running, two silhouetted figures,
Black against an eggshell sky,
Transfigured in glory.

CHRISTMAS MORNING, TWO A.M.

In the soft and silent darkness
A shadow shimmers its silhouette.
Awake, I do not stir
But locate the shapes:
Wardrobe, drawers and chair
That speak to me of home.

It's early, I know,
Still a time for sleep,
But childhood remonstrations
Return with comic force
"He doesn't visit boys who aren't asleep."
And "Only if you're very good."

Faint breathings, creaks and turning overs
A few hours before
This house will come to life
And like snow falling from the eaves
I breathe a sigh
For the ghost of Christmas past.

HINISH

Aftermath of marauding magpie
Raiding the blackbird's nest
Voracious, atavistic,
In our back garden.
Too cruel anywhere
Why do they do that?
Because they do. It's nature.
The inadequacy of words
While the distracted bleating of parent birds
Mocks our rational response.

Bouff!
Your word for waves breaking on the shore
Only at Bembridge Point they lap on sand and shingle
Cosying against sea worn silent sentry groynes
Performing their Solent vigil
Cloaked in bladderwrack brown.

And triumph. Your work carried home from school
A stanza on Autumn. The making of meaning
Bears, squirrels, flowers, the earth falls asleep
Undeterred, you find a rhyme for finish.

EDEN CAMP

Assaulting the ears
machine gun patter
 a siren's moan
whistling bombs, civilian shelling,
Vera Lynn, Glenn Miller swing.

The injured, the dead
statistics pile up to numb the sense.
Searching for answers
through ersatz smoke and blackout dark
anoraked kids hear the Feuhrer's bark.

Blitzed by this world at war
we emerge to a view
of waving crops, the Vale of York
and the line of the Hambleton Hills,
blinking in the light.

MY FEET ARE KILLING ME

(The Montgomery bus boycott of 1955 - 56 took place after Rosa Parks was arrested following her refusal to give up her seat to a white passenger.)

Some folks try to change the world
by marching armies overland
by taking elephants across the alps
and building navies for all to see.

Rosa Parks sat down and said
"My feet are killing me."

Some folks try to change the world
by parading on a pedestal
by saluting soldiers with their fluttering flags
and ranting and raving hysterically.

Rosa Parks sat down and said
"My feet are killing me."

Some folks try to change the world
by poisoning your mind
by spreading words of hate
and making victims flee.

Rosa Parks sat down and said
"My feet are killing me."

Sticks and stones
vilification
vile abuse
they were no use.
Why didn't they let her be?
Rosa Parks just sighed and said
"My feet are killing me."

VISITING POET

Holding up the spoon
we were asked to write
"Just a list of words."
What do you see when I hold this spoon?

At ease with my teacher's expertise,
I began to write.
I knew the score and didn't share
my charges' apprehension.

What do I see?
The spoon is unwashed,
a symbol of my dereliction.
Duty - stained and tarnished.
Thus have I measured my life.

While Joanne, tiny and almost mute
for three weeks now,
gazing at the spoon
saw the moon.

OUTLOOK FOR THE LESSON

A Ford lies on the school field,
the blackened, charred remains,
a testament of an evening's joy
riding the stolen gains.

The sharp winter rain intensifies
against the classroom pane
and neon flickers fail to lighten
the descent into lessons again.

Led towards attainment
Sandra finds a gleam
of comfort in her fantasy,
escaping into dream:

Cliff top walks, arm in arm,
spirits rising higher,
the flower that was picked for her
blooming in desire.

"Back in the land of the living?"
Effecting a complete success,
the tone is finely done -
crushed petals on the desk.

The clouds draw in.
There's the thump of a distant train.
The rain rattles and runs
against the classroom pane.

HALF-TERM DAWN

It will not always be like this;
The slow release of October frost,
The lawn reclaimed inch by inch
while crows flap in distant mist.

An early morning brew,
No sugar and a guilt-free taste,
Held to the view
Silence and a breathing space.

But it will not always be like this
The demands of unmarked books will grow
and shrill voices of jobs about the house
will clamour for attention.

Creaking floorboards above and curtains drawn
are active confirmation,
For now I sip and think
It will not always be like this.

VISUAL AID

Sun filters through the window
and clumsily drawn nets.
It is hot on this last week of term
and we don't want to work.
Not today.
Not today when the coming weeks
beckon with opportunity.

We are shown pictures
grainy images of barbed wire
across shrunken faces drawn taut
and he asks us to write
today.
Today when we are looking forward
to our tomorrows.

Rail tracks run to the distance
slowly closing on the narrow point
fading towards the gates of hell
and our tongues struggle with Berkenau
today.
Today when statistics lose any sense
and we no longer comprehend.

STRIPPING FOR GAMES

drenched with a full day
downpour muddy wet pitches
ready for games

we crowd the doorway
sir is late the pack await
ready for games

the changing room
cavernously echoes shouts
a key is turned

clamouring for first
we readily discard
shirt ties shoes

today the tribe will
glory in the chase
hunting in a pack

but in a corner
recidivist subversive
victim lacks excuse

fleeing life minute
by minute he knows the score
of dark approaches

tears long forgotten
not wanting to spoil our game
silence held on trust

battered abused
carrying the secrets of
predatory spoils

on the rain soaked pitch
the boys have games
innocence is drowned

MR BROWN WHO TEACHES MATHS

When the first rumblings –
a promise of terror to come –
were heard in the western sky
he felt a moment of dread.

A jet fighter passing overhead,
last lesson, Friday.
A chance to disturb the peace
too good to miss,

the deafening roar and foundation shake
would surely provoke a buffoon's retort.
But no.
His word held fast

and the mechanical exercise
carefully designed for killing time,
kept his class rapt
in head down furious labour.

Silence returned
the clock
ticked on
to the bell
and Mr Brown
who teaches Maths
dismissed his moment of dread
rather like
the blob of indelible ink
on the pocket of his shirt.

MR BROWN INVIGILATING

On a day
when dust danced
in the slanting rays
and several seasons since
resigning the mantle
of flannelled fool,
Mr Brown patrolled the aisles.

Duty dulled by routine
vigilance anaesthetised
by his charges' fevered hush
and a passion gently stirred.

For in the manner of an amputee
involuntarily scratching,
with his left elbow impeccably correct
Mr Brown placed his foot to the pitch
and caressed a ball
straight past cover point.

MELTING POT

Formula and periodic
elemental table, changing states
class 3B in the crucible
transformation waits.

Among a group of stupid boys
you, calling me by name
passing me the scissors
heated on a flame.

A frog for the kissing
but now I sit and wince
about paying you attention
my embryonic prince.

No place for alchemy
a lesson sadly learned
still ready to forgive
but I'd had my fingers burned.

YEAR 9 WITH FERGUS AS MY INTRO

Fergus allows the power of speech.
Speak of fears or dreams,
or of what really does your head in
then pass him along to the person on your left.

As cats go he's just a scrap,
a few ounces plus of felt and beans
stumpy tail, lifeless eyes
and four cotton whiskers that droop.

His provenance sadly, is a fast food chain
and a long forgotten burger campaign.
But if you hold him in your palm
you might find them eating out of your hand.

The empty space transformed.
Slowly peeling away layers,
learning from peers, pupae to pupils
emerging from uniform grey.

Except for the group of boys
who were going to resist all that
revealing the psyche
that treads on insects, kicks at cats.

They were nasty to you
weren't they Fergus?

OUT OF TIME

I often travel that way to work
and try the names out on the tongue
Ramsden's Bridge and Birkwood Lodge,
Bottom Boat and Fairies Hill.
Along the canal in the shifting mist
resisting years, the names endure
nineteenth century points on the map
bearing the burden of Yorkshire coal.

They take me too, to ply my trade
ferrying the value of words and names
articulating abstract loads
meeting locks and raising levels.

But against demand for the tried and tested,
vocational trainers' drills and skills,
it's an eloquent, empty gesture
like the Aire and Calder Navigation,
slapping against the banks
out of time.

THE HOLE OF HORCUM

Hunkered below the sill
Beneath the wind
Which blows *appassionato*
We sip our drinks
And think on scientific explanation;
Melt water and erosion
Carving and creating
Pigtrough Griff and Far Black Rigg.

But then demur
Preferring instead local lore
Of a giant seeking a place of rest
With fingers tensed
Like a monstrous claw
Bending to scoop
In one fell swoop
The Hole of Horcum.

TWO VIEWS OF ONTARIO MOOSE

I

They stand on every corner
drawing visitors in flocks
to pose and snap
and share the glory
of simply being there.
Toronto City celebrates
with a tourist rouse;
three hundred fibre glass moose.

Always getting his man
(and woman and child)
in scarlet attire,
there's the Royal Canadian Mounted Moose.
More soberly,
the university pays homage
to professor Moose-shall McLuhan.
Brightly painted,
there's chocolate and strawberry…
While outside the theatre,
Mama Mia!
There's Thank You for the Mooseic.
By the C.N. Tower, the Science Centre,
the harbour quays and Ontario Mooseum,
on the streets of Toronto
the moose are on the loose.

When evensong is sung a cappella
by distant wolves on hills
and evening lays its wreaths
of mist upon the lake,
summer heat dies.
And around the beaver created bogs
water lilies stir,
dragonflies dart
and mosquitoes draw their prize.
Here in the wilds of Algonquin
we look in vain for the moose
wading knee deep in brown, acidic water.
Reclusive, mythical moose
simply being that
disdaining urban hype.

BLOODY DONORS

Why not Kitchener's pointed finger?
Or at least his thumb and two neat pin pricks
for this is a noble cause
white feathers to those who make excuse

even their cars hector the unconverted
Drive carefully you might need me.
Here they gather, firm and resolute
shrugging it off as nothing

modestly keen to do their bit
the feel good factor rampant
leeching on the moral posture
Give and let live - more blessed than to receive.

Rhesus? Nothing negative about this
wreathed in sanctimonious self-satisfaction
in the Sunday school hall
they pass with barely a nod

The Life Givers
putting pictures of Jesus into the shade.
I am in donors steeped so far
that returning were as tedious...

It is as though they
and not the nurses
are giving me the needle
and I can t bring myself to look.

WALKING WITH GODDESSES

My mistress treads on the ground

Nobody's perfect
Tricky stuff this cross dressing
They know out there
I know
But in this sleeping compartment
We parade our night attire
All girls together
Playing jokes and jazz
For those who like it hot.

You know how to whistle don't you
Of course
It's just that at this moment
The quiet room, the tantalising smoke
The throat dries
It's never happened before
Honest.

Let's not ask for the moon
No quite
We have flickering images
Glittering eyes, pursed lips
And lying beneath tinsel
More tinsel
And
We have the stars.

For customers convenience
Please use the rear exit.
Fade up lights and credits roll
A torn ticket transfer
To the neon splash
Where crowds spill from doorways
And eyes don't meet
The litter strewn mean streets
Where a man's gotta do...

Of all the poems in all the world
She has to walk into mine
It could have been the start of a beautiful friendship
Is the message I never get to tell her
'cos in a swirl of fog and rotating propeller
she's gone
leaving Bogey and me on the tarmac.
Round up the usual suspects
My poem has been shot.

THE WORLD'S GREATEST LOVE POEM EVER (VOL. 3)

I feel it in my fingers
I feel it in my toes
There's a kind of hush
All over the world tonight
She may be the name I can't forget
Would you know my name
If I saw you in heaven
I can't take my eyes off you
How did I exist
Until I kissed yer
I'm crazy
Love, love me do
You know I love you
Until the twelfth of never
My girl
Every time we say goodbye I cry a little
There ain't no sunshine when you're gone
You're always on my mind
I can't live without you
I can't live with or without you
All I want is you
What a wonderful world
I believe for every drop of rain that falls
A flower grows
God only knows
It's all right now
Baby it's all right now
We may be dancin' in the dark
But I'm on fire
Pretty woman

When a man loves a woman
I get the sweetest feelin'
How sweet it is to be loved by you
I feel good
I knew that I would now
But I just phoned to say
Lay lady lay
I love you more than I can say
Some enchanted evening
Let's spend the night together
I'd like to make it with you
And I..I...I...will always love you
But will you still love me tomorrow?

A FREUD OF THE DARK

Being unable to run
In knee deep molten tarmac
When whatever it is
Gets bigger and bigger.

The sudden clatter of wickets
And the flurry for gloves and pads
And a box. Jeez, fancy forgetting that.
The urgent fumbling with thigh pad straps,
Whites around the ankles
And the omnipresent umpire
About to time you out.

Standing stark naked
In a public place
Announcing your shortcomings.

Falling

       Falling

          Falling

Inky black,
The water gets deeper and deeper
And there is less and less
Room to breathe.

MAN LYING ON A WALL

Of course, now and again
We'd all like a day off,
The toad work and all that…
But he lay there oblivious
As the church bells tolled
And the factory made its exodus.

To see him lying there
Brolly and briefcase neatly propped,
Freed from the cares of the office,
Fag pointing at the sky
And his hands indecorously folded
Above his trouser fly.

To see him lying there
Bowler on his belly
And his eyelids firmly closed.
A brick and mortar divan
The only support
My god, my god,
My old man.

BEACHED

Decaying rocks jag into boiling seas
lost children gulls cry,
the wind complains.
Waves invade, pulling pebbles
and sand towards the grumbling depths.
Insects bite and bleed a
black figure beaten by
the punishing sun.
Ringed by the horizon but still tilting
I'm king of this island.

King of this island.

FIVE ROAD ENDS

No longer fit for work
This is where he stood
Watching hours turn to days.

And if it rained
He stayed indoors
Reading again the Evening News.

He learned by heart
Births, deaths, local views
And who was up in court.

A week in Blackpool every year
Bed, breakfast, evening meal
And Boddington beer at night.

He'd been abroad just once
North Africa and an Italian beach
Which he never talked about at all.

DOMESTIC

He predicted that it would not rain.
It's not as if this cloud
spreading across the sky
like spilt ink
will not pass.

He observed her frantic bout
with the washing line
gaining a submission
over recalcitrant spokes
as the big drops fell.

He noted her return,
plastered hair, dalmationed shirt,
face flushed with the success
of saving washing from the line
and accusations about to break.

He rationalised inertia,
the rain - so sudden
like the first grumble of thunder -
and he reset his newspaper
predicting that this cloud will pass.

JUST ANOTHER SUNDAY

Difficult not to read into
this mess of unwashed pots
meaning
the detritus of a life
inertia.

He uses a spoon
to stir caffeine assisted courage
a serious radio station plays
pious invocation
Paschal incantation.

Later he'd find mindless music
but for now, over a radiator
arms spread-eagled,
a drying shirt
holds him.

Guiltily odds and ends
he shuffles into some semblance
order, discipline, ostensibly re-imposes
and the shirt
he casually removes.

PURGES

Fear of mice
or something worse perhaps
nesting prompted the onslaught
on that bottom corner
by the garden shed
where debris and windfall
fence panels had been stored
just for now and had lain
undisturbed for years.

The parade of festive relics
five in all
was unexpected skeletal
remnants of seasonal joy
with the nuance of each celebration lost
amongst a pile of rotting needles
and traces of ragged tinsel
we measure our lives with these denuded stumps.

When the roses
tangled stems heart shaped buds
were cut back
the void was filled with fog
smoke from the bonfire
curled and settled in desolate space
tools were packed away
mud was kicked from boots
we turned our backs
on these lean and haggard frames
in faith.

JOGGING INERTIA

Lying in the bath
I hear the last buzzing of mowers
on carefully tended lawns.

Distant kids recoil
from a call to bed.
Summer is at an end.

I drift in the steam
amongst clouded reflections
and running kit dumped after the vain pursuit.

Limbs ache towards another decade
while from the window, slightly ajar,
a breeze suggests a chill.

I am aware that I am lying
in the bath
and that soon I should make a move.

J. ALFRED MITTY

Sprouting wild, unchecked
grey hairs on the chest
are signs of machismo,
evidence of a life without
rehearsal:
doing and derring, buckles well swashed,
Hemingway posing
for his bullfighting kicks,
Flynn, swinging from the rigging
and Botham clumping an enormous six.

But fantasy like memory fades
(I'll never forget old whatsisname)
more and more grey hairs appear
and as the steam on the mirror begins to clear
the truth must somehow be told:
I shall soon be wearing my trousers
rolled.

SECOND CLASS POST

Amongst the bills, leaflets
and paraphernalia,
the picture postcard
glinted like a jewel.

Candy floss and funfairs
Bingo, fish and chips
Laughs, thrills and happiness
Greetings from a seaside town.

I knew you'd send a card
I knew you wouldn't fail,
I waited every day
and vetted the morning mail.

Your postcard came this morning
Glinting like a jewel
But all you could say was
"Wish you were here."

BANK HOLIDAY WALKING NEAR ASHBOURNE

"How often do you think of her?"
The girls ahead engage in chat
as we idly stroll by the flowing Dove.
Odd that he should mention that,
to choose this time, this place,
safely ensconced in coupledom,
to speak of love.

Indeed to speak of one
for whom a flame once burned much hotter.

Stung by this breach of etiquette
I pause. "Not often now..." I demur,
show apparent unconcern
and muse alone and with regret
how dying fires spark and burn.

BARGAIN BIN REMINDER

Held to inspection, face up
and then tilted at angles,
it shone, sparkling black in the light.
The fifty pence tag neither here nor there,
a trifle, a meagre sum for
years of denial of that other country
that lies behind.

And sure enough
paying for vinyl was exactly that,
a betrayal of stoicism borne over years
a rejection of this modern life
where compact discs triumph over long players
and the heart is concrete firm.

But blessedly free of fluff
and the irritation of crackles,
on playing, the notes were pure, production superb,
and each song so well remembered.
Alongside the singer songwriter's
rainbow of emotions

is the week we spent under sodden skies.
Every day a drenching. The Lakeland cottage
without t.v., no radio reception,
and one solitary album.
Playing now the lovelorn first track
I can still feel the rain
running down my back.

FRAMED SKETCH BY THE FRUIT BOWL

Lines to time
In awkward 2B
Framed beside the fruit bowl.

Separate paths, separate lives
But her smile survives
By one neglected pear

Eaten by decay.
Time denies
Hopes, dreams and lies

But the smirk at what is lost
Can not be ignored
These clumsy lines are deeply scored.

LOVE NOTES IN DISCORD

In the whisper of the wind chimes
stirred by the breeze
floating from the room where you work

and the upstairs tv
installed under protest
babbling from channel to channel.

In the constant buzz of traffic
pervasive and invasive
violating the moment,

the long lost weekend paper
arriving with a letter box slam
and a thud to the floor.

The steaming and hissing
tummy disorder rudeness
of coffee coming to the brew

and in the alarm call of a blackbird
fending off a crisis
are the words I won't say.

You emerge to the wind chime reprise
Paint-spattered, brush in hand
And smile.

As I do too
at Sunday about its business
in a major and minor key.

ECLIPSE IN THE PARK

Planetary forces
mysterious movement
vaguely concealed
by cotton wool cloud.

Minute by minute
the moon eats the sun
the diminishing crescent
turns day into night.

Silence wraps itself
around giddy kids
and earnest adult leaders
who ponder and point.

Searching for meaning
testing responses for something new
but we lack consensus
on our pinhole view.

SWEET THAMES RUN SOFTLY TILL I END MY SONG

Composed upon Westminster Bridge 3rd September, 2002.

Earth has not anything to show more fair
Dull indeed anyone passing this by,
Missing the site spread out against the sky,
The ancient laureate can still declare
The beauty of morning; silent bare.
Until rattling trains silhouette the sky:
Barging commuters; to sell or to buy?
Full of care, without the time to stand or stare.
Ignore the big issue, they seldom fret
About cardboard city where scroungers mill.
The city seat of Empire functions yet
Two hundred years of furthering debt.
On chartered streets the sun has long been set
And all that mighty heart is lying still.

MANOR POPLARS

Sunday morning
Walking through Manor Park
At every point of fascination we stop:
The garden where furtive rabbits feed in hutches,
The roundabout and swings,
A feather blown across enormous fields.
Father and son in acres of space.

But the greater silence is broken
Footballers tap a tattoo on the concrete path
Pungent with embrocation, they shout and cajole
Before taking sides.
In the final moments, paunches are held
And the last fags are stubbed.
The blast of the whistle
Transforms the pitch into a field of dreams.
A few mates, coughing in the morning mist
Are ready to serve as loyal support
And dwell on glories over a pint.

They stand before the poplar trees
Which bend and creak in the wind
Facing the years
Like old men on sticks.

THIS MOURNING BUSINESS

Following the ritual of grief
our front room is full.
These men,
these big men,
who carry authority and status
through labour and brawn,
now stand around at a loss
cloaked in cliche
and tentative display,
blocking light.

Rare emotion both tests
and re-asserts manhood.
I grasp the hand of my eldest
who strives to be hard in denying need,
claiming the rites of passage overnight.

The wind shrieks and branches
slap against the pane.
Fighting to come to terms
with what we are
and what we have lost,
my grip tightens
at the horror of tears
which I cannot shed
for now.

They call me Big Jim Evans
that's not how I feel
twenty years pulling the plough
keeping arrow straight lines
but now I can't dig deep enough
turning up words that say nothing at all.

Big Jim Evans swamped by a suit
as whispers ring the room.
What do I say to the eldest
arriving home from school?
Just stand and shake his hand
searching for the words I need
"It's a hard blow."
He stares back dumbly
at Big Jim Evans who can't find words
"A very hard blow" I say.

We like to do what we can
it was the very least
to pick up the lad from school
we would have liked one of our own
to deliver or receive
on that gravelled drive
load a case in the boot and pause
for the imposing view
uniform, tradition, assurance.
Not that morning of course
with such bad news
called from his studies
for the funeral of a brother
he hadn't seen in half a term.
A random moment, a random car
it could happen to anyone
but four years old...?
We said what we could
because you do
we like to do what we can
it's what we believe
but the death of a boy at four years old
told us again
it's not ours to give or receive.

LEST WE FORGET

The grumbling child is
quickly hushed
stiff-backed military youths
lower the flag
and for two minutes in
clerical reverence on Sunday
we remember.

Death
that we may live
sacrifice
to end all wars

And filing singly towards the altar
each one
swallows the old lie

CULLODEN MEMORIAL

Finished in Nairn
swimming, picnic and ices
Culloden was an off chance
something to do with time to kill.

Odd that we should find ourselves
deep in heather beneath dull grey clouds
thinking of sleet in April,
a diminishing dream, charismatic pretence
and butchery.

And how stones may last and flowers fade
after religion, ritual and vainglory
have driven men to fight.

MEMORIAL PLAQUE
(St Edmund, King and Martyr Church, Mansfield Woodhouse)

Voices of impassioned reason
Some of shrill dissent
The ebb and flow
Pulling and dragging
Pebbles in shingle.
Protection of minorities strikes a chord
But trumpet headlines jar.

Mark Royston Stephens
Ordinary Seaman.
Did he walk these streets
Stop these people for a light
And curse the Midlands rain.
What law or duty made him fight?

"For Freedom and Country."
It's little matter now
San Carlos Bay is his grave
The brass plate reads like
The cold slap of Atlantic wave.

IN MEMORIAM

Corfu, I remember
the battered bus driver's
devil-may-care
(Was he really called Stavros?)
The dusty verges where
garlanded headstones
tolled the victims
of ruinous road use.

And how at Easter
those whose grief stands testament
in flowers and stone
gathered for the celebration
of mysterious open-air Mass.
The triumph over death
marked with Orthodox passion
and fireworks flaring into the night.

Safely home
in England's grey rain
note too
the newly accepted view
how wilting blooms in cellophane
work their own miracle
enshrining lamposts and railings
yet decaying
like notions of the stiff upper lip
and not making a fuss.

STRAP HANGING

In the jostle for seats
they were separated
at each end of the carriage.

Braced against acceleration
and deceleration,
surfing the sudden swerves,
denied the joy
of secret smiles
and coded glances,
he hung by a strap
reading and re-reading
the poem on the underground.

She was caught in the crush
where eye contact is strictly taboo.
Someone leered down her blouse
pushed a cock against her leg.

DUTY BOUND

Interrupting the sofa and tele
of a Friday night
churning the miles
pulsing through
sheer volume of traffic
high speed fast food
inconsequential radio chat
travelling north

Testing responses at
the city walls
where everything has changed
and stayed the same
where flashing lights
dictate arterial flow
to the heart of town
birthplace re-entered
unrecognised

New pain new forgetting
inside an elegant
blackened stone façade
uniforms and efficiency
starched into action
journey's end in
a bewilderment of acronyms
overwhelming hospital heat
and beyond a row of
discreetly drawn curtains
the full glare

The last time I saw you alive
your black eye
in a sunken skull
glowering down the ward
accusatory
like a giant full stop.

THE END OF THE HOLIDAY

A good week agreed
our extended family holiday
picking at the tourist traps
a bit of this, a bit of that
castles, cottages and home made jam.
Or encamping on the beach
watching the channel's to and fro
where humpback ferries
come and go.
The hive and industry of kids
and to support an annual bond
their parents' unlikely sport.
Time drifting with the
pull and push of tides.
I skim through a broadsheet
while you, I know,
turn to *your* back pages
where *I* buzz the beach
and the cricket is for real.
In the evenings after dinner
we grumble about the beer
and talk about the weather again,
a thunderstorm, some showers of rain
but on the whole
you can't complain.

And today my father left
from grimy platform thirteen B.
We'd stay in touch
a letter when we can
unaccustomed to saying more.
A good week
but at the end of this holiday
the nights draw in.
I sit alone
dreading what the future will bring
the winter rain
and at some badly chosen hour
the insistent ringing of the phone
and inadequate words
inadequate words.

SHADOWS

You no longer cast the shadows you once did.
Your doctor, I imagine,
oozing professional expertise and practised bonhomie
put away the stethoscope,
patted you on the shoulder and said,
You never were a big fella anyway.

Sometimes they pass over graves.
We run from, hide in and emerge from shadows
and for years I lived in yours.
Odd that stature should be confused with physique
and odd that for all his medical skill,
a heartbeat strong enough
to withstand a Depression and a world at war
and to raise four kids
should fail to be revealed.

Hoping now to cast my own,
in the great business of knowing right from wrong,
of being strong, I no longer run nor hide,
I have no fear of shadows.
Except for the one you say
they found shading the lung
on your latest x ray.

AFTER THE STORM

After the storm
we potter,
random in our course
salvaging what we can
in silence.
Correcting, straightening, mending.
Building for the future
with minute careful tending.
And sadder, wiser, without hurry
we meet
tentative, reluctant to accept
the night could hold such fury.

ABOUT THE AUTHOR

John Clarke was born and brought up in Carlisle and is still emotionally tied to the fortunes of Carlisle United.

Armed with a degree from Leeds University and a post graduate qualification from St Martin's College, Lancaster, he taught in Hertfordshire, Nottinghamshire and West Yorkshire before his current post as Head of English at Balby Carr School, Doncaster.

His poems have been published in several magazines including Raven, Retort, Cutting Teeth, Smiths Knoll, Poetry Monthly and Asachi, a Romanian Arts magazine. "Manor Poplars" was a short listed poem in the B.B.C. Wildlife poetry competition.

His prose has been variously published. "Four Score Draws" was a Corgi Books Award winner and "I Was Ready to Fall in Love" was included in the Arctic Night anthology following the Featherstone Short Story competition. Several stories have also been broadcast on B.B.C. Radio. In addition, John's wry comments on the world of English teaching have appeared as articles in the Times Educational Supplement.

Further information can be gained from the web site: http://poetryjic.tripod.com

John now lives in Wakefield with his wife and son.